Mind Hacking

How to Unleash the Full Potential of Your Brain to Achieve Anything You Want

Mind Hacking

How to Unleash the Full Potential of Your Brain to Achieve Anything You Want

Unlock the Secrets of Your Brain and Become the Director of Your Own Life

Kyle Faber

Mind Hacking - How to Unleash the Full Potential of Your Brain to Achieve Anything You Want

Unlock the Secrets of Your Brain and Become the Director of Your Own Life

Copyright © 2018 Kyle Faber

All rights reserved. No portion of this book may be reproduced, stored in a retrieval system, or transmitted in any form or by any means – electronic, mechanical, photocopy, recording, scanning, or other – except for brief quotations in critical reviews or articles, without prior written permission of the publisher.

Published by CAC Publishing LLC

ISBN: 978-1-950010-09-7 paperback

ISBN: 978-1-950010-08-0 eBook

Contents

Introduction: The Untapped Potential of the Most Powerful Tool 10

Chapter 1: What Is "Hacking" Your Mind? 12

    Activity 1: Start a journal 18

Chapter 2: You Becoming the Director of Your Mind 20

    The "monkey mind" 20

    Activity 2.1: Observe the monkey mind 24

    Garbage in garbage out 26

    Activity 2.2: Observe the inputs 27

Chapter 3: The Mind's Codes 29

    "Buggy" code – how you got it 30

    Debugging the code 33

        Loops 33

        Habits 37

        Discipline & effort, resonance & momentum 42

    Eliminating unnecessary distractions 47

    If-Then loops 49

    Activity 3: Identify your habits, good & bad .. 51

Chapter 4: Fundamental Loops and Virtual Models.. 52
   Activity 4.1: Rooting out the fundamental loop: the "Why?" exercise... 53
   Virtual models, self & self-image 55
   Activity 4.2: Journal the gap between virtual and actual 62

Chapter 5: Beyond the Cognitive....................... 64
   The "extrasensory" you 66
   Activity 5.1: Breathe into Focus 68
   Hacking for "psychic" powers 69
      #1: Write it down 72
      #2: Talk less 72
      #3: Concentrate & pay attention 73
      #4: Wake up before 5 a.m............................. 74
   Activity 5.2: Concentration exercises............ 75
      #1: Observe and remember 75
      #2: Listen 76
      #3: Memorize... 76
      #4: Notice distractions 76

Chapter 6: Blueprinting Your Mind 78
   Activity 6.1: Journaling for a purpose............ 78
   Conflicting directions 79
   Blueprinting a new habit................................. 85

Activity 6.2: Journal for supporting values .. 86
Chapter 7: The Body's Contribution to the Mind 88
    The body's economy of effort and energy 89
    Activity 7: Gratitude hack 92
Chapter 8: Hacking the Tangible Brain 93
    The brain 95
    The cells of the brain 98
    Six hacks for the physical brain 100
    Your brain is only as good as what you eat .. 100
    Get more oxygen to your brain 104
        Breathe better 105
        Circulation and absorption 107
        1. Drink plenty of water 109
        2. Increase blood volume 112
        3. Work out more 112
    Sleep better 113
    Get some sunshine every day 117
Afterword 119

Introduction: The Untapped Potential of the Most Powerful Tool

A substantial part of human history has simply been about the human quest for ever more powerful and useful tools. Just think of all the things in the world that have been developed by the human mind. From harnessing fire to inventing the wheel, from Guttenberg's printing press to the Adobe PDF on your screen, so many human inventions, developments, and creations have been about creating tools to extend human abilities. Even AI, artificial intelligence, which mimics the human brain, is only another tool.

And yet, you already have the most powerful tool of all, the human mind. It has the power to create such advanced tools, and you already own one of those minds, but, like most, you probably haven't been getting the full benefit of it and what it is capable of. It's like walking into Harry Potter's wand shop on Diagon Alley and getting your hands on Professor Dumbledore's twin wand. Once you have the wand, you need to control it. And that is what "hacking" your mind is all about.

Your mind is the most powerful tool of all, or at least it has the potential to be. Mind hacking isn't about attaching an external electronic prosthesis to the brain and adding value to it from the outside. The mind has untapped powers that far exceed anything you could possibly contribute through any electronic attachment. Imagine what would happen if we spent the same resources to hack the human mind as we have in developing technologies and AI. The benefits would be significant and widespread. That's what we are doing here in this book. We are attempting to advance the potential of the human mind.

Chapter 1: What Is "Hacking" Your Mind?

Let me start by posing a simple question: What is *I*?

Before you think that's a typo, that I didn't have a good proofreader check my book, let me say, "What is I?" is precisely what I mean. And it's a very different question than "Who am I?" I'm not looking for you to provide a list of personal qualities or for you to define your identity.

So, let's ask it again. "What is I?"

I pose the question that way because you undoubtedly refer to yourself as "I." My question is simple – just what is it that you are referring to as "I"? If you want to hack your own mind, then the *you* that does the hacking is different than the *you* that is the mind that is to be hacked. This point can't be overstated. It is the key to everything we do in this book.

Imagine a car saying, if a car could, "I want to fix my engine," or a computer saying, "I will turn on." A computer that can turn itself on is one that is in standby mode on a different circuit whose job is to do just one thing – turn the computer on. In other words, the computer turning itself on isn't really the full complement of the computer turning itself on – it's turned on by a separate component sitting in the background.

When someone says they want to hack their own mind, it is not their mind that is saying that, is it? The mind can't possibly say it's going to hack itself. That would be like your computer hacking your computer. When you say you want to wake up at 4 a.m., who is the one that doesn't allow that to happen? When you want to go on a diet, who is suggesting that? "What is *I*?"

The obvious conclusion is that you and your mind are two different entities. *You* are not *your mind*. By picking up a copy of a book about hacking your mind, you are tacitly in agreement with that, although you may not have realized it.

You are not your mind. So, when I ask, "What is *I*?" I am asking you to think about what or who it is that you are referring to whenever you say, "*I* want this," "*I* love that," and "*I* want to hack my mind." Every time you say "*I*," just who or what does that *I* represent?

Let's look at this another way. If you are a movie buff, as I was when I was much younger, you know there are two kinds of movie-watching experiences. During one, you become so engrossed in the movie that you don't really detect the errors in logic or the bloopers. The opposite occurs when you can't seem to get into the movie, and you remain a spectator, observing from the outside. You see everything, not because you are a critic, but because you are seeing the overall movie. You haven't gotten into one character's experience or been pulled into the movie. I never notice the flaws in any movie I am truly engrossed in. But if I'm not interested, or the movie hasn't captured me, I can find all sorts of bloopers. Are you like that too?

When you are engrossed in the movie, you are *in* the movie, but when you are able to see all the little flaws and bloopers, you are watching *over* the movie. Do you get the spatial analogy? In the first kind of movie watching experience, you become part of the movie, you are *in* it, forgetting your actual physical location and becoming part of that movie's reality. In the second, you remain *outside* the movie, with a bird's eye view of all that goes on.

You and *your mind* have the same relationship. You become so engrossed with what your mind does that you think you *are* your mind, but you are not. You are simply caught up *in* the movie that is playing in your mind and engrossed by it. Most of us are so deep into our mind's perception of the outside reality that we don't realize the distinct difference between *the mind* and the *I*, confusing the two.

However, if you think that *you* can hack *your mind* – as evidenced by your interest in this book – that suggests that you do recognize their separateness, at least intuitively. Or you may be familiar with any one of the Old World philosophies or New Age practices that seek to highlight and teach the separate nature of the *I* and *the mind*.

Now that we have an idea of who the different players are in this endeavor – the *I* and *the mind* – we will be able to assign different roles to those players as we start working with the nature of the mind to "hack" it to do what we want it to do.

Hacking is a process and a method of *working around* the design, utility, and limitations of a tool.

Let me give you an example of what I mean by "hacking," as the term is used in this book. It's like taking out an angle grinder, and instead of using it as a grinder, jerry-rigging it to a stand and using it as a circular saw. That act of rigging a contraption to allow you to use the angle grinder in a way it wasn't designed for is what "hacking" is all about.

As it pertains to your mind, "hacking" is about getting your mind to do things the mind doesn't know it can do or isn't doing, things that *you* want it to do.

Your mind is extremely powerful. So is your brain. By the way, they are two different things. Later in the book, we will focus on optimizing the physical brain. For now, just know that the brain is the physical object, and the mind is built within that. *You* are distinct from both – *the mind* and *the brain*.

The brain can physically carry out the mind's directions by moving muscles, altering metabolic rates, and doing an untold number of other things just to make those directives happen. Consider the simple act of smiling. When the mind directs a smile, the brain sends signals to a bunch of muscles. Here are some of them:

- The *levator labii superioris* pulls the corner of lip and nose up.
- The *zygomaticus major* and *minor* pull the corners of the mouth up.
- The *levator anguli oris* assist in raising the angle of mouth.
- The *risorius* pulls the corners of the mouth to the side of the face.
- The *orbicularis oculi* causes the eyes to crinkle.

Your mind sends one instruction – SMILE. Your *brain* signals multiple muscles of your *body* to do their thing, none of which you are conscious of.

In the same way that your mind tells the brain what to do, and the brain goes about and does it, *you* can tell *your mind* what to do. *You* can decide to smile. In most cases, your mind will get to work and do it. But not always.

The mind is often referred to as a "monkey mind" as it takes off on its own doing random and seemingly incongruent things. There is nothing wrong with your mind – that is its nature – and that nature is, in fact, one of the reasons it is such a powerful tool. The mind's ability to associate things is, as the saying goes, a feature not a bug. It's just that that powerful tool needs direction.

Have you seen one of those cartoons where a fireman's hose gets loose and thrashes about uncontrollably with the sheer force of the stream of water coming out? No one would consider that stream of water to be useless. In fact, it is extremely powerful. But it has no direction.

The mind is the same way – it is very powerful, but it has no direction. That's where you come into play. *You* need to give *your mind* its direction, and when it doesn't give you what you want, that is when you might "hack" it to work around its natural design and limitations. That is what hacking your mind is about – getting that infinitely powerful mind of yours to do something you want it to do, even when it isn't complying or doesn't understand.

* * *

There will be practice exercises at the end of every chapter to help you build your ability to "hack" your mind and get it to do what you want it to do.

Activity 1: Start a journal

Get a notebook that you can write in as a sort of journal. Your first entry will be to write your answers to the following questions.

1. If you were able to enhance your mind, which of the following areas would you choose to improve right now (before reading this book)?

    a. Empathy

    b. Focus

    c. Resolve

    d. Discipline

    e. Foresight

    f. Creativity

2. If you could do whatever you wanted with $100,000,000, how would you spend it?

3. What three habits would you like to stop?

4. What three habits would you like to acquire?

5. What do you want your legacy to be?

6. What will your greatest achievement this year be?

Write your answers to these questions in your journal. Also record the date and where you were.

This exercise is just to get you started on thinking about what you really want your mind to be doing and the direction you want to go in as you start to hack your mind.

Chapter 2: You Becoming the Director of Your Mind

The "monkey mind"

Meditation counselors refer to the mind that wants to do other things when you try to make it concentrate or do something specific as the "monkey mind." You will agree that the analogy is apt as you picture a monkey erratically, excitedly, and unpredictably jumping from one branch to another.

The characteristics and behaviors of the human mind are determined by the brain that underlies it. We retain memories and store information catalogued against each other in the way that the brain is designed to do. Mental content is stored in the brain by connecting electrochemical cells (neurons) with each other, allowing you to associate things from one to the other very rapidly. Computers catalog things in serial order, whereas the human mind catalogs and stores them associatively, by association.

Therefore, there are two types of thoughts that roll around in your head, one willed, the other associative. Willed thoughts are those ones that you actively seek out, the thoughts that you bring up and direct. For instance, you might deliberately call up thoughts about the kind of birthday cake you want to surprise your spouse with. By contrast, associative thoughts occur when you happen to see a nice birthday cake with an ornament on it, and that reminds you of your spouse's interest. That triggers another thought, "Hey, maybe that'd be a nice birthday cake for my honey's birthday," and off you go on a train of associative thoughts.

The problem arises when you try to think of something deliberately, purposefully putting various thoughts together, but everything you do triggers unrelated thoughts. In other words, associative thoughts are getting in the way of the willed thoughts you are trying to direct. While the distracting thoughts may not be related to what you are trying to do, they are associatively related by the words and features of the issue.

For example, you could be trying to decide on a dish for dinner, and you think of having fish. That might trigger a thought of fingers (from fish fingers). From fingers you get to thumbs. From thumbs you get thumbs-up which looks like a "like" symbol. From the like symbol, you begin to think of Facebook, and the next thing you know, you're thinking of something you saw on Facebook.

From fish to a Facebook meme. Imagine that.

Sometimes, the associative train of thoughts is conscious, and you can see the progression, but, at other times, your thoughts are not conscious to you at all. They move under the surface of conscious thought. All you realize is that you're thinking of what's for dinner one minute and the next you find yourself checking your Facebook feed.

It's like the monkey in the mind jumps out at you, and yells, "SURPRISE!!" holding a bunch of shiny and interesting thoughts. Eventually, we can even become addicted to these random thoughts because they are interesting and unexpected. For many people, those unbidden thoughts can also cause discomfort, fear, or worry. Whether negative or positive, those thoughts are still distracting *you* from what you want to do, and can, therefore, be considered intrusive. Even a favorite neighbor who keeps surprising you with wonderful stuff can become annoying when you are trying to get the baby to sleep or trying to prepare your taxes.

Intrusive thoughts vary in intensity, frequency, and by the individual. Sometimes those intrusive thoughts get so loud or insistent that the original thoughts are overwhelmed and driven out. Even though you still need to think about getting dinner ready, your thoughts are now on something you saw on Facebook, and then onto other stuff you have associated with it in your own mind. All the while *you* are along for the ride. Meantime, you can't seem to get your head in the game to prepare dinner as you keep going off on the associative rides your mind keeps taking.

At this point, you have already accomplished the first step to get out of this. What you needed to know is that *you* are not *your mind*. It takes some effort, but, knowing that, you can step back from your mind to see it from that aerial view to understand all the things happening in your own mind as they happen. You can stop being an actor immersed in the scene and become the director who has the overview of the entire scene in the context of the plot and all the rest of the elements of the movie.

Once you get used to seeing yourself as independent of your mind, you will be capable of extraordinary things, some of which can even seem inspired beyond the ordinary cognitive powers of the brain. Your mind, under good direction from *you*, can accomplish amazing objectives. For that reason, recognizing that *you* are separate and distinct from *your mind* is the first hack and most important of this book.

Successful people have mastered the ability to step back and pan out. They see both the macro and the micro views. Those who aren't able to step back to observe the workings of their own minds end up resorting to strict discipline to try to get their minds to do what they need it to do. But that is the harder and less effective way to accomplish things.

You need to develop the ability to distinguish *you* from *your mind*. Of course, they merge back together easily, even automatically, as you would want them to. The goal is to be able to choose to be the director or the actor depending on the circumstance. So, the art you want to perfect is the ability to separate out *you* from *your mind* at will, allowing them to resolve back into "one" when you no longer need to be outside the movie of your mind. Both perspectives can be fun.

The best way to separate out *the mind* is to use a little mental jujitsu. The point of jujitsu is to use the momentum and energy of the opponent and flip it around on them, using as little energy of your own as possible. You can do the same with your own thoughts. You can use them to get your own footing and establish your point of perspective toward them.

Activity 2.1: Observe the monkey mind

Find yourself a comfortable spot. Sit down quietly, without any outside distractions or demands on your time or attention. One good time to do this is after the family has gone to bed. No phone, text email updates. Just you.

Close your eyes and let your thoughts fly. If you have nothing to think about, think about anything that happened at work or what happened with the kids or your friends. Anything!

Trigger a train of thought, any kind of train of thought, and, as the thoughts start to catch on, simply step back and watch.

Watch your thoughts coming and going wherever they come from and in whatever form they take. It doesn't matter if they are serious or fantastical, from aliens at Disneyland to mathematical equations or your neighbor's latest car purchase. It doesn't matter where your mind wanders. Just watch it. And tell yourself, "Hmm. That's interesting." But don't interfere with your thoughts. Don't egg them on, stop them, question them. Don't be affected by your thoughts one way or the other. Let your thoughts pop up like Whack-a-Mole – just don't take a swing.

You will find that this exercise will give you the best proof that *you* are not *your mind*, and that you are certainly not your thoughts.

Even though you can get your mind to think the thoughts you want to think about much of the time, you will still find your mind doing its own thing. Some folks will tell you that discipline is the key. But there are "hacks" that can help you work around this feature of your mind.

As you move forward, continue to do this sit-down exercise, letting your thoughts do what they want while you simply observe them. The key is for you not to participate in your thoughts. Remember that *you* are a spectator of *your mind* and that it is not you that is doing the thinking.

You should do this daily until you begin to easily see the distinction between you and your mind. When you do, you'll be able to start observing your mind in a way that is only possible if you are outside looking in, not when you are caught up in it.

Garbage in garbage out

The mind is like an echo chamber. Give your mind one sound bite, and it will reverberate into the farthest recesses of your mind. So, what is the best way to keep your mind echoing good vibrations? Give your mind good input material. The greatest limitations, by far, that the mind labors under are the inputs it is subjected to.

The mind is a powerful organ that connects the tangible to the intangible – thoughts to action – but the mind is only as good as what it is exposed to. In computing terms, GIGO (Garbage In Garbage Out), a concept computer programmers are more than familiar with. It means that computers are only as good as what is put into them. If you feed garbage into a computer (input), then you are going to get garbage out (output). The human mind is the same. If you feed it bad inputs, it won't give you the best outputs possible.

This is both the mind's greatest weakness and its greatest strength, depending on the inputs you provide it with. If you expose your mind to superior content and provide your brain with stable nutrition, then you will find you can take advantage of the mind's power. If you provide your brain with high glucose-based energy and expose your mind to poor content, then what you will have is a mind that performs erratically.

You and your mind have different command and control mechanisms. Your mind and brain together have evolved as highly competent command systems that make your body do what the brain commands. But you do not have a solid line of control over the mind. We tell it what to do, and when it compiles – great. But there are many times that it can't comply, doesn't know how to comply, or just simply won't comply. For these times, hacking is the solution.

It all begins by differentiating *you* from *your mind*. (Throughout this book, *you* will always refer to "you," not your mind.)

Activity 2.2: Observe the inputs

As you continue to observe the activities of your mind, observe and evaluate what you are putting into your mind. Your mind is molded by the experiences that you allow it to experience. Evaluate the kinds of entertainment you expose yourself to, the types of books you read, the movies you watch, the ideas you absorb, and the activities you take part in.

Write your observations and evaluations in your journal.

You'll know what to do to improve the inputs you provide your mind, if you think about it – for now, just remember that everything you expose yourself to influences how your mind develops and functions.

Chapter 3: The Mind's Codes

Once you get the hang of watching your mind's activity and observing the kinds of things it looks at, what it worries about, or what it keeps going back to, then you will start to really understand what is happening in your mind. Then, you can get to work hacking your mind to function at optimal levels to do all the things you want it to do.

You need your mind to make things happen in the physical world. Your mind is your tool for interacting with the physical world – in just the same way that your iPhone is your tool for interacting with the online world. Your mind provides you with its ability to interact with and extract benefits and experiences from the physical world. However, your mind does better when it has good direction from you. Without you, your mind is like that thrashing fire hose.

By developing your ability to step away from your mind, observing it separately, you will start to see the mind in its element, its real nature, and how it thrashes around without steady control. Then, by taking a "hacking" approach, looking for ways to work around its natural design, you'll be able to direct your own mind in whatever way you need.

"Buggy" code – how you got it

As you get better and better at stepping back from your mind to see it separately, you will gradually start to notice the codes that tell it to run in particular ways. However, most of the code written into your mind wasn't anything you consciously keyed in on some kind of ethereal keyboard. Most of your code has been written by experiences, culture, and what you have been taught – without you realizing it. But, just like the computer code that tells a computer to beep when a message comes in, codes can be altered to mute the incoming alert or raise its volume.

Your code is written by all the things that happen to you. Early in your life, what happens to you is the result of external influences. Heck, even your existence was not something you or your mind planned. The moment you come into this world, your code starts to be written. More and more code is written through the influence of your family, friends, TV, school, games, activities, social interactions, and anything else you experience. Some of those codes are buggy or conflict with other parts of the code. As you progress, the code becomes more complex, with more data and facts written into your memory. The rate of new code getting written and installed in your mind expands at an exponential rate.

And, finally, here you are. Fully coded, bugs and all.

Why is one man polite and another man is not? Is the rude man "bad" and the polite one "virtuous"? No. Why does one person get anxious before an exam, while their friend does not? Why does one person always choose the healthy meal, while the other binges on junk foods every night? The code that has been written into their brains dictates how they behave, how they think, how they interpret the world.

And if you remain passive, like the computer, more code continues to be written for you, outside of your awareness, by external forces, circumstances, and experiences. And that code will continue to have bugs, inconsistencies, flaws, and conflicts.

When a computer has a "buggy" program, the output has glitches, and sometimes the entire program crashes, and needs a reboot. In humans, that "bugginess" manifests as stress, breakdowns, anger, anxiety, and the general sense of being overwhelmed.

The people and experiences that contributed to your original code have faded into the background, while you are left standing independent with a mash-up of codes that give you conflicting perceptions, information, and feelings. You try to do something about it, but your mind is running on incompatible sets of code, and it won't let you get in and change it. You find yourself achieving less than you want, and what you do is unfulfilling. "Hacking" it is a way for you to work around your mind's limitations, the conflicting codes, and the obstacles it presents to change.

What can be even worse than code that dictates how you behave is code that dictates how you perceive things. That can result in unimaginable suffering. Your life traces an arc based on the decisions you make. You base those decisions on how you perceive the given situation or issue. The trajectory your mind takes from one experience to the next, your life today, and the opportunities that come your way are all rooted in the way you perceive what happens to you.

You need to sit with this idea for a minute. How you experience life is not at all about what happens to you, but about how you perceive what happens to you. That perception occurs in your mind. If you are *in* your mind (*in* the movie as opposed to outside watching it), then you only see what the mind sees, the perception that has been coded into it. If you are *above* your mind, you can see the bigger picture, that your perception of what happens is the result of the codes in your mind, and that, as the director, you can change it, create your own "director's cut."

Debugging the code

As you've seen, the first step to hacking your own mind is to realize that you are not your mind. Your mind, as powerful as it is, just runs the code. To be truly in charge of your own life, to be the director and programmer of your own script, you'll need to rewrite some parts of that code, but before you can do that, you have to take the "bugs" out of that code.

Loops

The mind works and thinks in loops. When those loops are subconscious, you will only see the outcome of the loop. When those loops are conscious, you can see them going around and round. This is like a computer that executes a program, or a section of code, running it in loops.

When my youngest child became interested in computers, he started off with programming microcontrollers. Those are little devices acting as a computer designed to interface with real-world physical objects. His first design was a sensor hooked up to his bedroom door to detect if someone came in. The code that went into programming his microcontroller had just three lines. Those three lines of code told the microcontroller to look for a break in the invisible laser beam that went from one side of the door across to a sensor on the other side. If you put your hand through the beam, it was broken, and the alarm sounded.

How did the code know how to know if something interrupted the beam? It asked. The three lines of code simply kept asking the sensor, "Did it break yet?" If the beam was not broken, the sensor would return a negative. As long as the answer was negative, the alarm would not sound.

That simple question was coded as a loop. Each time the answer was "no," the program would repeat the question until the answer was "yes." Then it would sound the alarm. It was an infinite loop that ran thousands of times per second, faster than you could decipher or interpret it, just keeping on asking the question (like my youngest son on a long road trip asking, "Are we there yet?") over and over.

And that is just how our brain works – in infinite loops, always querying, looking for a break in the chain, or a break in the sequence. Our mind is all about loops. It is an efficient and effective design, but it can also be one of the brain's greatest design flaws – when it works against us. Love it or hate it, it is what we have. The important thing is to figure out how to use it, or work around its limitations, in a word, to "hack" it.

If you still aren't sure what a loop might look like in a concrete sense, remember the last time you weren't able to get a tune out of your head, one that just played over and over. (At this very moment, I can't seem to get a 90's Britney Spears tune out of my head.) A song gets stuck playing in your head in a repetitive loop, sometimes for days. In a more debilitating example, individuals with OCD (Obsessive Compulsive Disorder) exhibit thoughts and behaviors that go in loops.

Our minds run, at the fundamental level, on loops and associations. Associations of the same thought can come around and around repeatedly, and if they are relevant, we pick up on it. It is a brilliant system, but it has flaws if we don't take control of it. Loops are everywhere. Even sleep runs on loops. Babies, for example, go through cycles while they sleep, with their bodies doing a periodic system check for hunger. IF the baby is hungry, THEN it wakes up crying.

Some loops are small and used for inconsequential issues. At other times, small loops connect up to form larger loops, and larger loops combine to become even more complex loops. Those complex loops are responsible for how the mind works. Loops and associations are really the bits and bytes of the human mind. Those loops can produce either good or bad results.

Being successful or unsuccessful, being happy or being broken in life, being ambitious, or being anything else are all kinds of loops.

One typical loop defines the potential your mind believes you have. If you were raised to think you have infinite potential, then, in your mind, you will have a loop that always tells you that you have potential, that you can do anything you want. If, instead, you were raised to think that you are worthless, then that worthless loop will play over and over in your mind, getting in the way of your success. It all comes back to a loop that was programmed into your mind a long time ago. And that is only one small loop.

Your attitude to failure and mistakes can be another small and persistent loop in your mind. If you were taught that mistakes were unacceptable, that'll be a small loop that keeps replaying just under your conscious thoughts. Then, when you make a mistake, you feel like crap. You feel guilt. Guilt leads to frustration. Frustration leads to anger, and as my master, Yoda, would say, "...anger leads to the dark side." Nonetheless, that loop plays continuously in your mind. Whenever you try something that fails, that loop kicks in, and eventually you may stop trying. Thomas Edison, you shall not be. As a variant that avoids making mistakes entirely, you may have a loop that doesn't even allow you to expend the effort unless the outcome is certain, a loop for the unwillingness to take risks.

There's a saying – "success is a habit" – and it's true. Success is a habit made up of loops. Potential is converted into action by attitude. If you don't care about making a mistake – and I don't mean the reckless kind of mistakes – then you can go all out. When you go all out, and you make a mistake, then you can pick yourself up and try again. With each try, you have more data about what doesn't work. But it is the sense of your own potential that allows you to keep banging away at it until you get to where you need to be. That's an attitude loop that encourages you to make an effort, fed by the loop that provides you with the sense of your own potential, and supported by a loop that lets you try again when you make a mistake. When you achieve a successful outcome and are rewarded for it, it creates an altogether new loop – one we describe as a "habit."

Habits

Habits have three component parts: a **trigger**, an **act**, and a **reward**. If you do something a few times when a specific condition is present, and you experience a reward for doing it, the mind starts to see the action as something you should keep doing when the trigger is present. And that's a habit.

We create all sorts of habits – some of them "bad." I have a habit with chocolates. It's a rudimentary habit. I feel down, I eat a chocolate, I feel good. The trigger is I feel down. Instantly, I take a chocolate bar from my laptop bag (I used to keep a ready supply of Mars Bars and Snickers in it). I eat it (the act), and I feel good (the reward).

Eventually, the habit just started running on autopilot, and I would automatically reach inside my bag without even realizing that I was feeling low or hungry. I even directed my assistant to keep my bag constantly supplied with Snickers and Mars Bars. Before I realized it, I had gained 30 lbs.

Habits can keep you doing something until you don't even realize you are doing it – and the next thing you know you've hit 30 lbs., or chewed off all your fingernails, or are up to smoking two packs a day. Habits can also keep you making successful moves – until you have achieved a successful outcome, graduating with a degree, building a business, writing a book, growing a garden.

Habits can be "good" or "bad" or even benign, depending on whether they help you or hinder you in getting what you want.

Habits are constructed from smaller loops nested inside larger loops. Some people reach for chocolate whenever they feel depressed. Depression is, itself, a self-reinforcing loop. When that loop runs, it triggers another loop, and then that triggers a reward that triggers another loop.

Loopy, right?

But this is good. Because we can work with loops. In fact, hacking your mind is all about working with loops. All you need to do is create a new loop for your mind to pick up on and the next thing you know it displaces the old loop. Whether it is eating unhealthy foods, smoking, or some other bad habit, you just need to displace one loop with another loop – and you can change your life. If it's a helpful loop you want to keep or a new one you want to create, you can struggle to complete that loop every time – or you turn that loop into a habit.

That's all attitudes are too – loops that become habits. If you have the right attitude, then you will put in a good measure of effort. When you put in the effort, without distraction, then you will win more than you lose. Winning and succeeding are, in themselves, an intrinsic reward. Suddenly, having the right attitude becomes a habit.

There will be some things that won't pan out the way you expect, but when you habitually put in your best consistent effort, most things you do will work out. When they do work out, you succeed, and you expand your sense of your own potential. With an expanded sense of potential, you'll find yourself having a better attitude, because you succeeded the last time. That, in turn, turns into super effort, and, when that works out too, you have an even better attitude and even greater potential. This is a positive self-reinforcing loop that has become a habit.

On the other hand, if you have a poor attitude, and you go into a situation, thinking, "This is not going to work out," then you are likely to quit before anything comes of it or you won't put in much effort, and you will fail. So, you announce that you knew all along that it was a fool's errand, and your attitude suffers even more. It's a classic downward self-reinforcing loop.

When you look at each of these scenarios, which of the self-reinforcing loops do you find yourself in more often? Do you mostly find yourself in positive loops or negative loops? Whichever you regularly find yourself in, it has probably become a habit.

If you are always operating in a successful loop, then you don't need to do any debugging in that area – unless you want to make it even better. But if the negative loop scenario sounds familiar to you, then you need to pause for a minute, examine the loops you find yourself in, and ask yourself some questions.

Looking at a downward or negative loop that runs in your life, at what point in the loop do you think you can break the downward spiral?

Can you break that spiral at the potential loop, the attitude loop, the effort, or the outcome?

Of course, your ultimate goal is to change the outcome – that's the whole point. But the outcome is not where you can make the change; you need to change something that can lead to the better outcome.

Of course, you also need to have the potential for doing it – but that's not so much about what you have as it is about what you perceive you have. If you believe that you have the potential, then you will have it, but if you believe otherwise, then you won't – it's a loop. In my experience, everyone has potential. When I look at anyone, I see potential, even when they don't see it in themselves. No one has zero potential. They may temporarily lose it, misplace it, or forget how to access it, but everyone has potential.

So, in breaking that downward spiral, that leaves attitude and effort to focus on. You need to be able to put in a wholehearted effort in whatever you are doing and that requires the right attitude. Attitude is in the mind, and, while effort is expressed through the muscles, it begins in the mind. And since attitude and effort are found in the mind, they are hackable, and where you should apply your changes.

How do you get over a habit? You replace it with something else. That is how many people quit smoking. They get a patch. The patch replaces the nicotine while eliminating the physical act of smoking. Once the act of smoking stops, half the battle is won. This is the replacement of one loop with another loop. To get rid of a negative loop, you need to displace it. The best way to debug a bad habit is to replace the loops in the habit with different new loops. The habit is dismantled – one loop at a time.

And remember habits themselves are loops. Change a few of the loops that make up the habit, and the habit will change. Replace any of the loops in the habit, and the habit is disrupted. Better yet, replace all the loops, and you have a brand-new habit.

That is how you debug a habit, and that is essentially how you debug any part of the overall code.

All of code in your mind is made of loops. Change any loop, you change the code. How do you change a habit? You replace it – one loop at a time.

I used to have many addictive habits. I liked having habits, because they provided a sense of predictability. Do this, get that. And I avoided changing any of them, because I used to think that to change a habit you needed tremendous discipline.

Discipline & effort, resonance & momentum

Discipline is really a kind of a loop of its own. **Discipline** can generally be understood as using effort to do something, working against the forces opposing it. Discipline can be the hard way to do things. But it doesn't have to be that way.

When discipline and effort are used to install a new or different loop to replace an old loop that you want to get rid of, it becomes difficult when the new loop is out of sync with the rest of the things going on in your mind and your life. Discipline is often used to force an outcome through effort, working against opposing forces. However, discipline can also be used to work with existing forces to amplify the effort expended.

Imagine trying to punch a large sand-filled punching bag at the gym. Newton's Law of Inertia states that a body at rest tends to stay at rest. Right? So, when you strike that first blow, you're going to move that bag a little in the direction of the punch by the sheer force (effort) of your punch. If, instead, you strike the bag when it is coming toward you, what happens? Or, if you hit the bag on its swing away from you, what happens? Striking the bag on the swing away from you sends it the furthest of all because you are working with and adding to the existing momentum, whereas striking it when it's on its way toward you will injure your wrist because you are working against momentum.

The same goes for discipline. You have to "jujitsu" it around, rather than using blunt force efforts to force something to be the way you think it should be. You should apply your effort when the tide is with you, moving in the direction you want to move, not when the tide is against you.

Resonance occurs when you apply effort or force at the right time, which magnifies the effort. Using discipline to apply force at the wrong time diminishes the effort. But, remember, discipline can also be used to apply the effort when it produces the greatest effect.

As an illustrative example, let's look at my experience with the addictive habit of smoking. I used to smoke two packs a day. The brightest part of my morning was lighting that first cigarette. When my first child was born, I had to cut back, having fewer opportunities to smoke after we turned the house into a no smoking zone. Studies were exposing the dangers of second-hand smoke. Worse, the smell of smoke in the air, on clothes and drapes, predisposes kids to smoke later in life, so we decided to keep the house smoke-free.

I made the effort to get to work earlier just to get my first morning smoke, and I stopped at the gym on my way home from work to shower and change into a fresh set of clothes. This went on for two years.

However, my child was a precocious two-year-old, and one day he asked me, point blank, what the odd "stinky" was that he smelled on me. I had thought I did a good job of getting rid of all the traces of smoke, but a non-smoker can always pick out the smoker because the smell is so strong.

I came clean about my smoking, but my son couldn't understand what it was all about. I didn't want to sing the virtues of smoking to him, so I couldn't say much, but he grabbed hold and wouldn't let the subject go. One day, he found a pack of my cigarettes, and the picture on it horrified him, so he began pestering me to quit. Try explaining the concept of addiction to an almost-three-year-old. You can't.

I felt I had no choice but to quit. And I did it cold turkey. That was the last time I smoked – twenty years ago. I did it the old-fashioned way. I put in all my effort and stoked up the discipline to get the 40 cigarettes a day addiction down to 0 in one afternoon. I sat, that night, at my desk without a box, pack, or any cigarettes in the house. It wasn't bad yet, because I was still at home where there were no triggers, since I hadn't been smoking at home for three years.

But I knew my office was going to be a trigger-rich environment. So, the next morning, I called my assistant and told her to cancel or postpone all my meetings for the next week. I stayed away from the office and had contractors go in and renovate my office. I left instructions for what needed to be done. Then my wife and I packed up our child, and we went on vacation for five days. Drastic? Yes.

But, remember, we talked about triggers, actions, and rewards as the components that form a habit.

Places can be triggers. Events can be another kind of trigger. So, instead of fighting the flow, the momentum of the habit, I stepped away from it and reduced my exposure to the triggers. Then, all I had to contend with was the nicotine withdrawal. (I didn't use nicotine patches.)

To debug my smoking habits, I altered my surroundings, my schedule, and my triggers. In essence, I got around the habit, hacking it, in order to change it. As many as possible of the loops that I had that were associated with smoking were displaced by new loops and new triggers during that week away in the mountains. I ate more, drank more coffee, and just hunkered down – and relied on good old discipline whenever those proved temporarily inadequate.

As my experience with quitting smoking shows, changing loops and habits is a holistic affair. Not only do you need to change the loops themselves, but you need to make those changes in a way that doesn't clash with the established movement and momentum of the things around it.

When you try to energize the swing of a pendulum, you can't do it when it is on its way toward you, that is, when the momentum is against you. You need to wait until the pendulum has begun to swing away from you. Then your effort will be aligned with the pendulum's momentum, and you will achieve what you want.

Otherwise, you just mess up the harmony of the swing.

If you already have an entrenched habit, don't go into battle with it. You want to change your habit, not beat yourself up while you are doing it. The habit is more likely to win a direct battle.

Certainly, if you put enough effort into anything, you will see results, but combine that effort with a hacking approach, and you will see the effort-to-reward ratio tilt in your favor. Successful people know how to do this, even make a habit of it, getting into a loop "on the ground floor," where the momentum is working with them and then just give it 110 percent.

Eliminating unnecessary distractions

An important thing to tackle in debugging the code in your mind is unnecessary distraction. Distractions are both a coding problem, and an obstacle to debugging other parts of the code. Rooting out distractions is an art and takes years of practice. First, we need to define what a distraction is, and then we need to look at the type of distraction.

A distraction is anything that crosses your path that is not immediately necessary for the task at hand. If you are watching a movie, a text from a dear friend, no matter how close, is still a distraction. Calling your mom, while she is grading a student's essay, is a distraction for her, because you aren't part of grading the essay. Some distractions are acceptable, even welcomed. Other distractions are not.

If you're trying to get your taxes done, and it's 30 minutes to midnight, the most delectable ice cream and movie by the fireplace is an unwelcome distraction. Much of the time distractions are appealing, because we want to do the thing that is more fun than what we have to do. Other distractions are annoying, because they interrupt the thing that is more fun or more urgent.

Either way, the clear problem is that, once there is a distraction, our minds are rendered inefficient.

Hang on a sec... my son wants to play chess. Will be right back....

Okay, I'm back. See, some distractions are more pleasurable than others. But they are distractions nonetheless.

So, we need to categorize distractions. Not every distraction needs to be expunged from our life. Some distractions can give us meaning and purpose, or even give us a much-needed boost, so that we can get back to what we were doing before, renewed or better in some way. There are times when the mind is exhausted with what it has been doing, so it seeks out distractions. That allows it to get away from the matter at hand and provides the opportunity for a higher inspiration to work on it in the background.

The distractions we especially want to control are the ones that appear in our mind unbidden and are so engrossing that we forget our intentions. The distraction that takes us away from something we want to accomplish often operates on some kind of loop.

If-Then loops

A person who is easily distracted is typically someone with a faulty If-Then loop. Or probably more than one.

In coding computer programs, one of the most popular kinds of loops is the If-Then loop. An If-Then loop is used when you want the code to do something dependent on something else. The code tells the computer IF this condition is fulfilled, THEN do that action. When you place that in a loop, the loop runs until the condition is satisfied, and then it does the action it is programmed to do.

The brain has its own If-Then loops running for almost everything you are involved in. One simple loop is this: IF energy levels low, THEN feel hungry. Not elegantly stated, but you get the point. Even fear runs on If-Then loops. IF this happens, THEN feel afraid.

For distractions, one of your If-Then loops might be: IF you are feeling frustrated, THEN seek out stimulation elsewhere. Or perhaps the If-Then loop may be: IF a friend calls, THEN drop whatever you are doing. There are thousands of possible variations.

What you need to do is find the IFs and the THENs in your own loops and evaluate whether they are warranted or helpful. You also need to identify the root loop – the fundamental loop. In the next chapter, we'll be talking about how to get to that fundamental loop.

You must do this carefully. If you remove the wrong If-Then pair, the consequences can be catastrophic. You can apply this, for now, to distractions, and even then, be cognizant of what you are doing.

Erasing the "bugs" in your own loops will change the way your mind triggers different cognitive, visceral, and emotional responses. If you are someone who has anxiety issues, then you will find that hacking your loops will make a lot of difference in the way you handle your mind, your body, and life in general. Changing the loops can help with anger issues, procrastination, self-sabotage, fear of speaking, and any of an almost unlimited number of issues.

The one who eliminates the "buggy" loops, by the way, is *you*, not your undirected mind, not some outside force. If you need to erase certain sections of the coding in your mental loops, you do that by displacing them. It is too challenging and limiting to try to eradicate a loop without putting something else in its place. So, replace a faulty loop with a loop that is beneficial.

But just how do you replace a faulty loop? You need to start by identifying what you want to change.

Activity 3: Identify your habits, good & bad

List all the habits you have, as many as you can think of, small and large. At this point, don't worry about whether the habits are bad or good. Just identify as many as you can.

Next, make a separate list of things you think would make your life easier if they were habits.

Go back to your first list, and identify the ones you think are good habits and the ones you think are bad habits. Then write down why you think each one is good or bad.

Chapter 4: Fundamental Loops and Virtual Models

This chapter will give you two important ways to identify and better understand what is going on in your mind, so that you can work with your mind instead of against it. The first is a technique to dig down and discover the root of a loop. The second is to understand the virtual world you have been building in your mind.

To accomplish the first, you will learn a new practice that will help you understand why your mind does the things that it does. This technique is taught in Ivy League business schools but is not always practiced in big companies. The ones who do, though, seem to stay on top.

Activity 4.1: Rooting out the fundamental loop: the "Why?" exercise

This is an easy exercise, designed to get to the root of anything. All you need to do is ask a series of eight questions, and, usually, you will get to the bottom of the matter by the time you get to your eighth answer.

Here are the questions:
1. Why...?
2. Why...?
3. Why...?
4. Why...?
5. Why...?
6. Why...?
7. Why...?
8. Why...?

No, I'm not trying to be funny. Kids do this all the time, but we either take it for granted or get cross with them. Yet, it is the way the mind naturally works, using a loop of asking for a reason and justification for every answer. How else can you get to the bottom of things? Children instinctively have it right. When you apply this strategy to the contents of your own mind and to the things it does, you can slowly start to see the mind's own foolish (or brilliant) ways.

Pick one of the bad habits you identified in the last activity which has been prevalent in your life. Apply this simple procedure of asking "Why?"

repeatedly until you have no place left to go. Here is the way it might go.

1. Why am I always late for work? Because I don't like going to work.

2. Why don't I like going to work? Because I might be criticized by my boss.

3. Why would I be criticized by my boss? Because I doubt that I'm good at my job.

4. Why do I doubt that I'm good at my job? Because I don't think I learned it well.

5. Why do I think I didn't learn my job well? Because I am not a good learner.

6. Why am I not a good learner? I don't know, but my teachers told me I wouldn't amount to anything, because I don't have the ability to learn.

That was done in six questions. Saying that you need to ask eight questions isn't really an accurate statement of what you need to do to get to the bottom of the subject at hand – it's just a convenient estimate. Sometimes, you will be able to do it in six, but, other times, you may need to ask "Why?" many more times.

The point is to go down the rabbit hole that each answer creates. Before long, you will start recognizing and identifying loops that are active in your mind. You will find that some loops are just absurd. Nevertheless, they reside deep within your mind at work in your mental programming.

Virtual models, self & self-image

In this book, we have really been dealing with various forms of the self. The *"I"* directs the mind, while the mind has the responsibility of managing the body and the reality around it.

Many people are entertained by the antics of their own mind. The moment their mind takes off on one of its associative flights of daydreaming, they sit down to watch the movie, relishing whatever the mind has to offer. These mental movies and antics are, in fact, the basis for the great power of prediction that the mind has. That power begins with the mind's ability to create models.

To hack our own minds, we've already been discussing how *you* (the subject) are viewing *your mind* (the object). The object and the subject are two very different things. The object, in philosophy, is the thing being observed. The subject is the one that does the observing. For example, if you are looking at a ball, the ball is the object, and you are the subject.

Now, we need to take that one step further. The mind operates within a neurochemical organ, the brain, and it needs to make a neurochemical replica of whatever it sees, hears, feels, smells, and tastes, in other words, of whatever it observes. To be able to understand how the object works and how it responds, the mind needs to make a virtual replica of the object in the mind.

In the late 20th century, research scientists came up with a new way to test things. Before, when someone wanted to test something, they had to go out and run a test with the real object. For example, they had to build a test plane and actually fly it to understand how it would operate under real world conditions. They still do that, of course, but more selectively and not as often as they once did, because now aerospace engineers also use a method known as *non-destructive testing*. It uses computational models placed into computational environments where a computer calculates and predicts how something will behave in any given situation.

That is essentially the same way that your mind predicts its own encounters with its environment. In your mind, there are different models of objects and environments. Every time you interact with an object, those models are updated to increase the accuracy of future predictions.

Imagine, if you will, taking a drinking glass and dropping it out of a third-floor window. What will happen when it hits the asphalt? Can you imagine the result? Of course, you can. Is the result the same if the glass lands on the grass? If I, now, asked you to imagine dropping an object made of the latest material, Napherene, would you be able to see, in your mind, what happens when the object strikes the asphalt? No. The reason is that you don't know the properties of Napherene. (Napherene doesn't exist.) Because you don't know what Napherene is, it has never been subjected to your senses or your reasoning faculties, and so you have no model of it in your mind, and you don't know how it will behave in the environmental model in your mind.

We spend our entire lives building up intricate models of environments, objects, incidents, people we know, events, ideas, and everything else we experience. Brand management is an entire field built around this idea. A brand, logo, trademark, color, jingle, or buzzword are designed specifically to evoke a model in our mind of an experience of a product, place, or promise. That model gives us the sense that we can predictably know what will happen (with the product, place, or promise) as we interact with it in our mind's mockup.

There is one more element in our mental mockup that we haven't yet talked about, and that is the model of our own self. In our mind, we have a version of our self, of who we think we are. This is what we can call the "ego." To get a better result from hacking the mind, we need to take a closer look at the ego in this virtual environment.

Although we often refer to someone who has an over-inflated view of themselves as having an "ego," everyone has an ego. For this book, don't confuse the ego with something that makes you act obnoxious, with being conceited or "egotistical." The ego we are talking about is not an ego that is over-inflated or thinks too highly of itself.

For our purposes, the ego can be understood as a software version of the person. It is a replica created in the mind to model its own interactions with the world to have better experiences or better outcomes. But a lot of problems can arise with this. When the replica is not consistent with the real-world manifestation, conflicts can occur. Imagine what could happen if your virtual replica, your ego, is able to bench press 300 pounds, but your real self is only able to bench press 80 pounds.

Think back to that model of the glass falling from the third floor as you imagined dropping it. Who, in your imagination, is it that does the dropping? Who holds the glass out the window? The mind needs a model for the actor in that scenario. A sane person would visualize themselves as themselves instead of visualizing themselves as Arnold Schwarzenegger. Such a discrepancy could cause some real real-world problems.

So, just how close does the virtual model come to the real thing? The model that you make up in the virtual world impacts your real-world life in two ways. Either it can help you to create outcomes that are exactly the way you intend them, or it can have you living in an "alternative reality."

Imagine that you have a completely unrealistic model of yourself in your virtual world, and you encounter a situation where you think you can do something that you can't. Suppose that your ego has been built up to believe that it can swim the English Channel, from Calais in France to Dover in England, and you jump in to swim the English Channel, but your body doesn't know how to swim. What happens? This extreme example demonstrates how the virtual self in your mind can be inconsistent with your real self in the physical world. However, that inconsistency can work in the opposite direction too. Sometimes your virtual self (your self-image!) is incapable of doing something that your real-world self would be perfectly able to do, if only given the chance.

Another version of the problem can arise if you have an inaccurate view of the environment you are in, while your virtual self is accurate. Imagine that you are on the moon but don't know that the moon has less gravity than earth. Based on earth "data," you believe that you need to apply a certain amount of force to jump two feet. But when you act on that model, your jump propels you much higher than you expected, because the environment on the moon does not have the same gravitational pull, and that was not part of the model you were acting from.

The point is that there are two worlds – both are equally real. One is the realm of physical reality. The other is a virtual reality in the mental realm. You can stand back from this virtual reality, stepping in and out of it to see things from different perspectives.

Another way to get a better understanding of this concept of a virtual model of a person's self is to think about a narcissist. A narcissist is a person who has a wildly exaggerated view of himself in his mind's virtual world. Unfortunately, as things grow increasingly inconsistent between how he sees himself and the realities of his actual self and the world and its reactions to him, there is a disconnect that causes damage to his ego. Instead of correcting his virtual self, the narcissist uses others to validate his inaccurate view of himself. To get that validation, he masters the art of manipulation, so that he can get what he is looking for, validation of the virtual self that exists only in his own mind. In other words, the narcissist tries to force reality to conform to the virtual version in his mind, instead of revising the faulty virtual self-image.

Unlike the narcissist, when you understand how you interface with the world around you, you can start to make improvements or adjustments to your own virtual world and to your self-image.

The more you experience the world around you, the better you can predict outcomes, because your virtual world gets closer to the truth of the physical world. You can "hack" your mind by starting to pay attention to the things around you, so that you make better models in your mind. Those better models will, in time, allow you to make better predictions about what you can do in this world, and increase your contribution. That will increase your happiness, and who knows, that may even increase your wealth and stature as well.

There is a strategy that has been advocated across the motivational genre which is to pretend to be who you are not (yet) in order to become that person. You hear it in advice like, "Dress for the job you want, instead of the job you have." If you can control how far you take it when you follow this kind of approach, then it can work fantastically. But the key is not to deviate so far from reality that it starts working against you. At its worst, it can even start becoming an unhealthy delusion.

If you are a senior executive at an investment bank, it's okay to dress up like a CEO. But if you are working in the mail room, dressing like the CEO could be problematic. The distance between the model you create of yourself and how you need to be in "reality" should be closely managed. This strategy is not about having good feelings from pretending to be someone you aren't, but it is about getting into the frame of mind where it is possible to become the new person you want to be. It's about opportunities for growth.

If you keep the gap between reality and your virtual world tight, then you can reap the benefits of having a useful model to work with. But if the gap is too big, then the conflicts between the code and reality will work against you and what you want to achieve.

Activity 4.2: Journal the gap between virtual and actual

Do these two writing exercises in your journal.

1. List times that you expected you would react to something in a particular way but didn't.

Pick one and use the "Why?" question technique until you uncover the fundamental loop that caused the discrepancy between the way you expected to react and the way you actually reacted.

2. Describe your virtual self in detail, not based on "real" evidence, but based on how you see yourself. Describe the traits, ideals, beliefs, and values that you believe you have.

Compare that virtual "you" with your actions in the "real" world.

For example, perhaps you consider yourself an environmentalist who wants to preserve the rain forest because you believe climate change is a real danger. Do your actions rise to the occasion? I firmly believed that I was a proponent of the environment, and I believed the science behind it. But I was caught off guard when I audited my own virtual self against my reality self. I started to notice that my actions (the ones that benefited the environment) weren't voluntary, and other possible actions that weren't compelled were not done. That was a wake-up call for me.

Do you have any areas of your life where you think of yourself in a certain way, but you are not acting in a way that is consistent with that self-image?

Chapter 5: Beyond the Cognitive

Your mind is extremely powerful, capable of running many different loops and nested loops (loops inside loops) in every kind of situation. But that's just talking about cognition, the brain, and how the brain controls the physical body. You have capacities, however, that go beyond the sensory-based cognitive capabilities of the mind. We all have them, but not all of us use them.

The difference between the normal cognitive abilities of the mind and the extrasensory "psychic" capabilities boils down to the ability to concentrate in different modes. And guess what? Concentration is really just another loop.

First, though, understand that concentration is something very different from meditation, although many people confuse them because they can feel like the same thing. Let's talk about why that is.

Think back to the beginning when we talked about separating out the *you* from *your mind*. When you do that, it's like watching a movie from the outside, but when you are stuck in the workings of your mind, it is like being in the movie. Imagine being Tom Cruise and watching the final edited version of *Mission Impossible*. He acted in the movie, experiencing it from the perspective of being inside it, and then he is watching it, as a spectator, from outside of the movie. Get it?

When you step back from your mind, you can still see it doing its thing, thinking, cogitating, raising random thoughts. *You* can observe it. But you are not *in* it. So, when you can observe it, you can also stop observing it. But your mind doesn't stop performing its functions when you stop observing it. It continues to do its tasks. But you have stepped back and stopped observing it.

What do you get at that point?

Silence. You get complete and total silence. The cognitive ability of your brain is still going in full swing, but it is silent as far as you are concerned.

By contrast, meditation changes the frequency of your mind's activity to the point where the thoughts your mind generates and its cognitive abilities are completely slowed down, so that what you are able to see is a relative silence. Meditation literally changes the physical functioning of the brain itself.

That is why meditation and stepping back from your mind can feel the same, even though they are not. One creates a relative silence while the other creates silence. In time, you should be able to do both, but, for now, what you need to do is to simply step back, separating yourself from your mind.

As we have already talked about, all the "hacking" of the cognitive mind that you need to do can be done from that vantage point. As you step back, you can make the various changes to the loops you want to alter. But that just addresses the cognitive abilities of the mind. The loops, habits, and associations are all tools of the cognitive mind.

However, there is a part of you that can be more than cognitive. It is something that all of us have, but distractions tend to block us from being able to access it. That is the part that you can access when you learn to step back from the mind and concentrate in such a way that you no longer hear it, and you discover silence.

The "extrasensory" you

When we talk about being "psychic," we are talking about getting input from outside of the five senses that we are normally consciously aware of. Sight, sound, taste, touch, and smell are all dimensions that you can attach to the memory of a specific object or experience to give you a sense experience profile of it. That is the realm of your mind's cognitive ability.

When you look at a plate of buffalo wings, fresh out of the kitchen, you can smell it, see it, feel it, taste it, and perhaps even hear the sizzle. The profile you get from the plate of hot buffalo wings comes from five senses. That is a cognitive experience of the buffalo wings.

However, information that hasn't come from normal sensory experience, those five senses, is referred to as "extrasensory," and usually assigned to the realm of the "psychic."

Extrasensory abilities rest with *you*, as opposed to the cognitive abilities that rest with your *mind*. We all have those extrasensory abilities, but we don't always know that they are there, and we don't know how to access them. That kind of "psychic" ability is the mirror image of cognitive ability. It is what inspiration, imagination, and connecting with the universe and powers greater than ourselves is made of. That is why, if you try to analyze it with cognitive tools, you can't. Yet, we all know there is more to our "self" than a cognition machine.

Any inventor or forward thinker – like Edison, Einstein, Newton, Steve Jobs – has mastered the ability to go beyond mere sensory perception, reaching into the extrasensory to see what others do not. Einstein's math wasn't as good as you might expect. That's not where he excelled. He was an average mathematician, but Einstein had insight into the universe that was more than what the cognitive brain is capable of. Einstein is considered a genius because he could ask a question in his cognitive mind, and get inspired answers. None of that is simple cognition. That is inspiration. That is a "psychic" ability.

You, too, have extrasensory abilities, but to tap into them, you need to be able to fully separate yourself from your mind, not only to observe it, but also to silence it.

So, it is part silencing the mind, and it is part separating your mind from *you*. There is no suggestion that Einstein was doing something like this consciously. However, it seems likely that it would happen when he was intensely concentrating. And that provides a clue into the nature of the abilities that we are calling "psychic." They require you to hold your concentration and separate your mind from yourself, while keeping your mind quiet at the same time – which allows you to access what is outside normal sense experience, the extrasensory.

Activity 5.1: Breathe into Focus

This activity is a simple one, a focused breathing exercise. All you need to do is breathe naturally and focus on observing your breathing.

Use your breathing to create a rhythm and point of focus for your mind. You are developing a habit for your mind. A loop. Get your mind to focus on your breathing without controlling that breathing. Let your body breathe at its own pace. You are just an observer.

This exercise will help you to develop focus and concentration.

Hacking for "psychic" powers

Most people believe in one way or another that there is more to the life than what we can perceive through our five senses. What we are calling the "psychic" you is the part of you that can perceive what the senses cannot. When you start tapping into the extrasensory dimensions of your mind, your insight into things increases exponentially.

Since the goal is to hack the mind, you will also want to be able to hack the extrasensory dimensions of the mind, so that its powers can also be brought to bear on the universe around you. Fundamentally, the qualities of the "psychic" mind are all about the speed and concentration of the mind, and the extent of the mind's development.

When I was a kid, my dad could tell when I was about to do something that wasn't allowed. I could have sworn that he could read my mind. Then I found that my mom was even better at reading my mind. I found that my grandparents and all the other elders were "psychic" too. It was super weird.

But as I grew up, I started to notice that I, too, began to develop those "psychic" powers until I was able to look at my daughter and see the ideas rolling around her head. I knew my daughter so well that I could just look at her face or the gait of her walk and tell how she was feeling, what she was thinking, or what she was about to do.

Super weird, right?

It was then that I realized that it wasn't that my parents or family were witches or anything like that. They could tell what I was thinking, simply because they understood the way the mind works, and combining that with my character, they knew what the outcome would be. It's like watching a movie and knowing what the ending will be half way into watching it.

This is indeed a super-natural ability. When you get to a point in your life that you have practiced concentration and you have created enough associations in your mind, you begin to see patterns.

Life is all about patterns. Have you noticed how the same things keep happening in your life in similar ways over the course of time? There are patterns and loops in the grand scheme of things and it works out that we always come back around with a second chance to do various things.

It's not that you get a second chances at things like a first marriage or the way you interacted with your parents (those are time-stamped and specific), but the skills you learn and the ways you can use those skills keep coming back around in your life. The faster you learn them, the quicker they can be used to move on to the next level.

If, on the other hand, you keep making the same mistakes every time an issue comes up, you can start descending deeper into chaos and difficulty until you learn what you need to change that pattern. It's like a video game. If you don't get the firing sequence just right, or you don't get the clues right, you get busted back down to the current level.

In the same way, you learn more, and the brain gathers more information, taking in more than you can consciously realize. The more you absorb, the more your insight grows – at an exponential rate. It's not just about data points. It's about constructing your virtual world so well that, eventually, you will be able to accurately predict what happens as a result of the actions you take.

Remember we talked about the virtual models of world and the self. Your mind can become so proficient at creating a virtual world modeled on the physical world that the more data you absorb, the more you can game out scenarios deep into the future and get predictable results.

And that power of prediction is "psychic" if you ask me.

So, just how do you develop that kind of "psychic" mind that can see into the future?

There are four things that you can do to start developing the beyond-cognitive powers of your mind.

#1: Write it down

Writing things down has the unusual capacity to affect the way you process the ideas and information that you write down. Part of it, of course, is simply the focus required to write down a coherent thought compared to the fleeting quality of a thought passing freely through your mental landscape.

When you write stuff down constantly and consistently, it materializes. Write down the things that you want to achieve. Your mind will start to notice the things that it needs to get you to that point.

#2: Talk less

The easiest mind hack that few ever mention is simply to stop talking. Talking less is not just about keeping quiet, it is also about not thinking about what to say next.

When you speak less, the mind conserves resources, not just in the effort it takes to talk, but also in the resources it takes to think. Have you heard that when a person loses one of his five senses the other four are heightened? It isn't that the remaining senses are intentionally heightened, it's that there are fewer input streams to contend with.

The brain is constantly receiving data from the five senses. Visual data goes to the visual cortex, sound from the ears goes to the auditory cortex, smell, touch, and taste all go to their respective cortices. Once interpreted, the data is sent on to the hippocampus for evaluation and memory formation. All that mental activity consumes a tremendous amount of resources. If you want to hack your brain, the best state to be in is a silent one.

#3: Concentrate & pay attention

Concentrating and paying attention is different from observing. Paying attention is about concentrating. We seem to concentrate a lot less these days, since we have data streams from everywhere chiming away in our pockets. Paying attention is taking one stream of input and not allowing yourself to be distracted from it. If you are in a meeting, turn off your phone, and politely ask that the other person does the same. Keep your time precious. Don't allow someone else to waste your time while you sit and idly wait while they spend half their focus with someone on the phone.

In everything you do, do only that. Break any habit of doing more than one thing at a time. Concentration, when it becomes a habit, gives you the power to look deeply into things, so that you will be able to use the increased ability of your mind to predict correctly, to have foresight.

The best way to concentrate is to pull your mind away from things that are intellectually stimulating and allow it to focus on what it is doing in the moment. If you are reflecting, then don't do anything else. If you are reading, stay within the four corners of the document. If you are playing, immerse yourself in the game. This is an old strategy, but it works very well when you are working to build up your concentration muscles.

When you make concentration a habit, you create a loop that goes something like this: Concentrate. IF concentration is broken, THEN discard distraction and return to concentration. Keep that loop running in your head, so that the loop automatically returns you to concentration each time you break concentration for a distraction. In essence, it's a loop designed to snap yourself out of it every time you distract yourself.

#4: Wake up before 5 a.m.

Waking up early is one of the most common habits that successful people have. If you are sleeping late because you are burning the candle on both ends, then you are damaging your health. Otherwise, you are simply missing out on the power of the morning.

Getting up before everyone else and having the time to silently get to all the things you need to focus on allows for 110 percent effectiveness. It sets the tone for the rest of the day. It's like getting a morning workout. Your body's metabolism peaks and stays high for the rest of the day. In the same way, your mind gets going and doesn't stop for anyone.

Early morning is the best time of the day for the highest intensity of thinking. Your mind is clear because it has rested, your subconscious has had time to chew on your queries, and you are full of answers and ideas at this time. The successful person is one that is filled with ideas and the energy to advance those ideas. To hack your mind, it requires the kind of clarity you can get when you wake up before 5 a.m.

Activity 5.2: Concentration exercises

Concentration exercises will help take your ability to extinguish distractions to a new level. The more you push the envelope when it comes to concentration, the more you will be able to see "behind the veil" of anything that is not readily identified or detected by the senses in the present moment of time.

#1: Observe and remember

You can do this exercise wherever you are if you are sitting still. Let's say you are on the train to work. Observe your surroundings without any thought in your head. Do not comment to yourself, judge, or get caught up with the thoughts in your head. Simply concentrate on observing everything that you can.

Then, later, in the evening, take out your journal, and write down everything you can remember.

#2: Listen

Listen to a piece of classical music and try to identify all the instruments being played.

Or sit quietly in the park or at home and listen to the sounds in the distance. Don't pay attention to the sounds around you or in the room. Ignore nearby sounds and noises and listen only for the sounds coming from a distance, locking onto them for as long as you can.

#3: Memorize

The next time someone gives you their phone number, take a good look at it, and try to memorize it.

#4: Notice distractions

As you read the remainder of this book, write a "+1" and the page number in your journal each time you lose your concentration. By writing it down in your journal, you are forced to notice and keep track of how often you are distracted. Over time, with practice, you should notice that you are becoming distracted less often.

Chapter 6: Blueprinting Your Mind

Hacking your mind, like hacking a computer, takes coding, practice, the power of observation, and something else....

Every hacker worth his salt starts off with a plan, a flowchart. If you think of hackers as guys in hoodies in a basement, banging away on computer keyboards backlit in red, think again. Some of the most sophisticated hackers sit in brightly lit buildings, attend strategy meetings with tier bosses, and work with flowcharts that resemble flowcharts for a manufacturing process. The hacking process is structured and meticulous.

Like a hacking campaign, to hack your mind, you need to start with a blueprint of what you want and how you are going to go about getting it. When you hack your mind, you need to have a clear purpose.

Activity 6.1: Journaling for a purpose

Get your journal out and write down all the possible reasons you can think of for wanting to hack your mind. No one else is going to see this journal, so feel free to pour your heart out in point form and get to the root of your purpose. This is your first step. We all have different reasons. From those reasons arise the strategy.

1. Why do you want to hack your mind?
2. What do you think it will do for you?
3. What level of achievement do you want to reach once you have hacked your mind?

Once you get to the root of your purpose, then you have clues to what is missing.

Next, ask yourself, "What is the greatest drain of mental resources that you are facing right now?" Is it financial? Is it family?

What is the greatest thing that, if removed, would allow you to focus at 100 percent?

What is stopping you and what might trip you up as you move forward?

Of course, you are hacking your mind to have a better life. You are hacking your mind so that you can leap ahead and make all those buckets of potential materialize and start paying off.

The journal is a way to create a blueprint of your mind. You can't really hack your mind effectively until you get all your thoughts laid out so that you can understand what your mind has been doing. You need to see the script of the movie.

Conflicting directions

I recently spoke with a talented artist who had been holding off on selling any of her paintings. I asked her what her goals were when it came to her art pieces. Her initial response was that she wanted to be recognized for her work at some point in the future. Fair enough, we all want to be recognized, not for the glamor and fame, but because being valued and appreciated is one way to gauge our contributions in the world.

My next question was to ask her to put a dollar value on her art. Without hesitation, she said, "A million." I admired the confidence and the goal. But, as soon as she said that, one of her conflicting loops kicked in, and instantly, without missing a beat, she said, "I know, that's too high. I guess I could settle for 10 grand."

There were obviously two separate loops running, one of wanting to strive to have a high level of acceptance and appreciation for her work, and another pulling in the opposite direction that it was unacceptable to set her aim so high.

We all do that. There is one side of us that wants to succeed, and there is another side that is unsure of our abilities. Until we resolve that conflict, we are just going to spin our proverbial wheels while we languish in indecision. Within our mind, the two loops are running against each other like a four-wheel drive vehicle with the front wheels spinning forward at full speed, while the rear wheels head backward at full speed. Although it may be producing a lot of smoke, that vehicle is going nowhere fast.

As you "blueprint" your mind, you will start to see where the inconsistencies are, where inaccurate assumptions, distractions, influences, and misunderstandings have become part of your mental coding and have created the incoherence that holds you back. When you take the time and devote the attention to lay it all out in your journal, you will gradually begin to clear those up.

As you lay out what is in your mind, you will start to see that your mind has just been doing what it knows how to do. Your mind is a function of its temporal, spatial, and social environment. What you have put into it, what has been put in for you, and what has simply accumulated has molded your mind into what it is. The functioning of your mind has been shaped through associations, loops, and habits.

While you are blueprinting and inventorying the contents of your mind, remember not to judge yourself or beat yourself up over what you may find. You are not a bad person. At worst, all of us are confused on many different levels. Often the original intention was good, but the consequences become undesirable, especially when conflicts between accumulated codes starts to occur. You have probably heard the saying, "The road to hell is paved with good intentions." That certainly applies here to the years of mental content that has built up in your mind. That is why you need to take the time to lay it all out and look for the inconsistencies and bugs that make your mind – and life – crash.

Just know that you cannot achieve this overnight. It takes time to journal and ferret out the bugs. But what will surprise you is that once you decide to clean up the inconsistencies, and you start journaling, you will see things more and more clearly.

Blueprinting removes the blinders, fallacies, and inconsistencies in your beliefs and automatic assumptions, giving you the opportunity to choose one path or the other. The point is not what path you chose but that you chose one. When you have a purpose, then your "hacking" becomes more useful. If you don't know the direction you intend to go, then you have no way of knowing what to correct, or worse....

Some time ago, a major airliner crash killed hundreds. The accident investigation eventually determined that there was a design flaw in the fly-by-wire system. Fly-by-wire was a new development in flying technology where the pilot's inputs were interpreted by the computer, and then the computer would send the signal to the servos to the control surfaces (ailerons, rudder, elevator and such) to get them to move the amount needed to execute the pilot's intent. If a pilot wanted to bank left, he would shift the joystick in the cockpit left, and the computer would sense that and adjust the ailerons as necessary to execute the bank.

That crash was inexplicable because the pilot had flown straight into an obstruction. It turned out that, while the captain was banking left, the co-pilot was trying to bank right. The computer read both signals and they had canceled each other out. The plane didn't alter direction and slammed into the obstruction straight ahead.

When you don't sort out which beliefs or values you hold, or whether your beliefs and actions are consistent, you will find yourself on a path that does not take you anywhere. You need to pick a direction. Bank left, or bank right. Trying to do both will drive you straight into the side of the mountain.

Doing the "Why?" exercise, found earlier in the book, will help you work your way through all the different sorts of loops in your mind – loops of actions, loops of values, beliefs, and interpretations. It will help you to identify just where your mental programming has inconsistencies and discrepancies.

Hacking your mind isn't about turning yourself into some sort of superhuman. It's really about shedding inconsistencies and discrepancies so that you can pick a course and concentrate on all the things you need to do to reach your goals. It's about identifying conflicts in the code, so that your mind can keep you flying in the direction you want to go, instead of crashing.

You will find that distractions provide some of the biggest conflicts in your mental code. You want to do one thing, move in one direction, but a distraction has you paying attention to something else, steering you in a different direction. Distractions come in all shapes, sizes, and forms, whether it is a movie in the mind, a compelling news story on the TV, or friends who keep posting cute puppy pictures on your social feed. You need to step away from distractions, one and all.

Whether it's an addiction to a substance, an addiction to a television series, or simply an addiction to distractions, you need to remove those vicious loops, but you can't remove them until you uncover them through your journaling. Once you do identify them, you can work your way down to the fundamental (root) loops, and then displace them one at a time.

Once you have done that, the blueprint process is easy. As you are creating your blueprint, remember that *you* are not the same as *your mind*. You are the subject who is looking at your mind. Your mind is your cognitive ability, and your "psychic" mind is the part of you that is adept in the virtual world – the part that gives you insight into the future.

When a successful person looks at an endeavor, they can foresee what will work and what won't.

For example, someone like Warren Buffet can anticipate the future of an investment. His faculties are so highly tuned that he knows exactly what an investment is going to do; when he picks out the features of an investment opportunity and puts them into his finely tuned virtual world, he can anticipate what it's going to do without doubt and hesitation.

To be able to foretell the future, your virtual world and your virtual you needs to be as close to reality as possible. If you don't like what you see, then go out and change that in the real world, and then update the virtual you. Doing it the other way is possible, but it is always better to simulate it inside, but work it in the real outside.

One of the most credible ways to move the mind in the direction you want is to change your action. The change in that action instantly produces results, and those results are experienced as a reward. Pretty soon the act becomes a habit.

Blueprinting a new habit

One of the most important tools in the blueprinting process is to establish clear actions and clear rewards. Say, for instance, you want to start a new habit of exercising every morning at 5 a.m. You need three things, a trigger, an act, and a reward. When you have all three in place, and you have repeated the loop few times, it will become a habit that you will no longer need to compel.

So, in this example, if you want to create a habit of doing a routine morning workout, place a trigger in your room – your gym clothes, perhaps. So, the moment you wake up, you see it sitting on the chair. Pick it up, get changed, and get to your workout. As soon as you are done, give yourself a reward, something you really like – something that you do not always have or that you don't normally consider – perhaps a milkshake, or a delectable slice of fruitcake. It doesn't matter if it cancels out the calories you burned during the workout. Your real objective is not the calories, it's establishing the habit.

When you have rewarded yourself, and your mind has locked onto the habit, then you can stop the treats. By the time your mind realizes that the sweets are no longer forthcoming, it has already started to experience a different sort of reward, the reward of better energy and feeling better from the morning workouts, so the sweets will no longer matter. Now you've created a new loop in your blueprint.

Activity 6.2: Journal for supporting values

Writing in your journal, list the values you hold.

Look for loops that express those values or that hold a value in place and write those down.

If you are having difficulty, use the "Why?" question technique to dig down into your value system.

With that done, identify and make a list of goals that you want to achieve.

Tackling one goal at a time, identify and list the values you hold that promote the achievement of the goal and the values that prevent it.

Decide whether the values that oppose your goal are worth keeping. If they are not, create some new loops to replace the ones you no longer want to keep.

When you finish one working with the values for one goal, move on the next.

* * *

As you start to lay bare the workings of your mind in your journal, remember that it is always going to be a work-in-progress. There will always be changes, new realizations will pop up, new habits will form, new situations will arise, and so on. So, keep your journal vibrant and dynamic. You are never the same person two days in a row. As Heraclitus said, "A man never steps into the same river twice; the river is never the same, and neither is the man." So, keep updating it, and keep referencing it.

Chapter 7: The Body's Contribution to the Mind

Now we come to the body. Just as there are representatives who sit in the U.S. House of Representatives to make the needs of the American people known, the body has representatives in the brain to make its needs known to the rest of the mind. The primal parts of the brain, in particular, are designed to look after many of the body's needs.

In many programs of advancement, we are told to disregard the needs of the body and advance the needs of the mind. Many religious practices and theologies teach that the body is sinful and the soul is to be prioritized. But hacking the mind is really about making sure that there is harmony between the mind, body, and the spirit, so that all parts have the opportunity to reach their full potentials.

The advancement of one does not have to be to the detriment of the others. There is a way to build them all up without taking a zero-sum game perspective. In fact, an optimally functioning and healthy body can help to build the mind and spirit. A powerful mind can help to build and mend the body and advance the spirit. There is a powerful feedback loop connecting body, mind, and spirit. Working together, they all play a role in fulfilling your needs and goals.

For the body to be an active part of the mind's game, the body needs to be as vibrant and healthy as possible.

The body's economy of effort and energy

The body (via the primal parts of the brain) is a highly experienced economist. The body's only currency or resource is energy.

Effort is the ability and intention to overcome hesitation. A body at rest tends to stay at rest, as Newton said. To move that body, energy is required. That energy is a scarce resource. The reward sought for using that energy is more energy. So, if you expend the effort, the body looks to get back more energy than what has been used.

For example, suppose that there is a store a mile away. You need to walk there, and it will take you 1,000 calories to do it. Your mind knows this (or thinks it does) in its virtual platform. But it also knows that there is free food there (or something else that will make it worthwhile). It realizes that, when it gets there, 1,200 calories will be waiting for it. Do you think the body will be motivated to get here? Yes, of course.

The body (or, rather, its representative in the brain) finds the answer to this "problem" by considering three areas:

1. How accurate has the mind's virtual world been in the past about these kinds of things?

2. How many calories are waiting versus how many calories need to be expended?

3. What is the opportunity cost of not doing anything?

If this sounds like a class in Economics 101, it is – it is just an economics of the body, and the mind has mastered it over time, as long as your virtual world is accurate – and that depends on you.

If you have been completely accurate in your assessments of efforts and payoffs in the past, then, when you consider making one of these trips, the body is going to weigh your analysis of the matter and score your endeavor. If it thinks that you have been 100 percent correct in the past, then it will award you a 100 percent weight to the first question of predictability and history. If you have been poor at predicting these things, then you get maybe 50 percent.

Now you go to the next question and look at the calories that need to be expended versus how many stand to be gained.

So, instead, let's say you get 50 percent for the first question. It takes you 1,000 calories of effort and there are 2,000 calories waiting. That means that at 50 percent of 2,000 calories, there are only 1,000 calories waiting for you, and you need to spend 1,000 calories, so the body determines that the benefit is a wash.

After that, the qualitative question of opportunity costs is factored in. This can take into account a broad range of other things, such as the opportunity to meet up with friends or the chance just to get out of the house.

Then, the body makes the decision. If the decision is to go, then you feel enthusiastic and motivated. If the decision is not to go, then the body feels lazy and hesitant.

This applies to every situation. There is always an economic analysis at the bottom of it. What the mind can control are the factor inputs. If you have been accurate in your analysis in the past, then your body is more certain of what is to come. If you have been prone to exaggeration, the body will take that into consideration. It's always good to not exaggerate.

But now, let's say *you* really want to go, even though the body is feeling lazy. That's where you'll need to hack your mind so that it can get the body to do what *you* want, to go to the place where the reward is waiting.

Whenever you feel lazy about doing something, realize that your body hasn't calculated the payoff in the way you do, and you will need your mind to pull the levers to make it happen. In most cases, the mind will take the side of the body, so you'll need to hack the mind to make the body do what you want.

When you want your body to do something, you to have to play a long-term game with it. You have to make sure that you never complain about the things you initiate, and, more importantly, you have to make a habit of being grateful and thankful for the things that you get. This will convey the message to the body that what you want it to do are things that it should be enthusiastic about doing.

Activity 7: Gratitude hack

In your journal, review all the loops you have identified, and, instead of criticizing the bad loops that you believe are ruining your life, praise the good loops. Leave the bad ones alone, and, instead, be grateful for the loops that make you do well. You can displace the bad loops later.

This activity is about hacking your brain with praise and thanksgiving. Praise your positives and be grateful that you have them. It's like getting a child to do well in school. If you praise the child for all the things they do right, you will find that they do right more often, and for self-motivated reasons instead of having to be bribed to do something.

Chapter 8: Hacking the Tangible Brain

How you move, how you eat, what you eat, and a whole host of things affect the physicality of the brain, and all of that has an impact on the effective functioning of the mind. Understanding how the physical brain and body affects your mental functioning will help you hack your brain to bring your mind to a new level of effectiveness. And the healthier your physical brain is, the more impact all your other mind hacking efforts will have.

It is common to talk about the brain and the mind as if they were the same thing, confusing them. They are, however, two separate things. The brain is what you find when you look inside the cranial vault. It has mass, shape, volume, weight, and all the other things that trigger sensory perceptions. In other words, it is tangible.

The mind, on the other hand, is not something you can pick up, slice open, look into, or otherwise handle in any interactive sort of way. The mind is intangible. However, the mind's intangibility does not make it any less real than the brain. Both are equally real, but different manifestations of existence. One is tangible like a pebble on the beach; the other is intangible like the force of gravity.

This universe is composed of two balancing phenomenon - all things are either tangible or intangible, and they always exist in pairs, like the brain and the mind. Planets around the sun are tangible, for instance, but the dark matter and space between those celestial bodies is intangible. Throughout nature, this balance between tangible and intangible is inextricable – when one exists, the other is there as well – you just have to find it. They are not opposites; they are symbiotic. A living person is made up of a tangible body and an intangible life. Without the intangible, the body is lifeless.

This is also true of the human brain and mind. The brain provides the structural and physical presence – the tangible side of the story of human cognition – while the mind is the intangible side.

A lot of what you want to do and who you want to become depends on your brain. In that balancing of the tangible and intangible, to have your mind functioning at its best also requires that you make sure your physical brain is functioning at its best.

So, let's turn our attention to the physical qualities of the brain.

The brain

The brain is just three pounds of gray and white matter. The gray matter consists of neurons and is about 40 percent of the brain, while the other 60 percent is white matter, consisting of dendrites and axons, which are responsible for the transmission of data. The brain has the consistency of a wet custard and is 60 percent fat by volume and 75 percent water by weight.

The brain can consume as much energy as a 20-watt light bulb and uses 20 percent of the blood flow in a person's body. All those resources reach the brain via a vast and intricate web of blood vessels. There are approximately 100,000 miles of blood vessels involved in the supply and return of blood to and from the brain. The brain is a resource hog, consuming more resources than any other organ of the body.

The brain has three functional areas, the cerebrum, cerebellum, and the brain stem. The **cerebrum** is the largest and is further divided into four lobes, the frontal, parietal, temporal, and occipital lobes. The **frontal lobe** is responsible for a vast array of human thought and action. It plays a major part in motor function, memory, judgment, and impulse control. It is also responsible for social and sexual behavior. The **parietal lobe** is where sensory information like taste, touch, and pressure is processed. The **temporal lobe** holds the areas of language comprehension, hearing, long-term memory, and the ability to recognize faces. Finally, the **occipital lobe** is involved with the interpretation of visual stimuli.

The **cerbellum**, located at the back of the head below the cerebrum, is responsible for movement, position, and coordination.

The **brain stem** is the most primitive part of the brain, responsible for the maintenance of automatic survival functions, such as breathing, heart beats, and more.

There is, of course, much more to the brain. The lore that we use less than 10 percent of our brains is patently false. We know varying amounts about specific areas of the brain, but, for the most part, science still has a long way to go in objectively mapping our brain and understanding how it behaves.

For now, here are a few of the major areas of the physical brain.

Cerebral Cortex. This part of the brain is where conscious thought and intelligence is processed. It is instrumental in our ability to remember, pay attention, and remain self-aware. It is the outer layer of the cerebrum and is made up of folded gray matter.

Corpus Callosum. The two cerebral hemispheres of the cerebrum are connected by one bridge that allows data to flow between the two. This is the corpus callosum.

Ventricles. Four pockets filled with cerebrospinal fluid are located in the center of the brain mass. The fluid which is produced in the ventricles cushions the brain, distributes nutrients, and collects waste.

Thalamus. The thalamus is located alongside the ventricles in the center of the brain mass between the two hemispheres. It is responsible for pain management and sensory detection.

Hypothalamus. The hypothalamus regulates the metabolism, manages the autonomic functions of the nervous system, and controls the activity of the pituitary, indirectly controlling body temperature, thirst, and hunger.

The brain's functions that have thus far been mapped by western medicine have been strictly based on physical representations of cause and effect. This means that, when they were mapping the brain, they would test an area to see the effect and would consequently map that function to that area. Each person has to be mapped individually using an MRI conducted with appropriate stimulation, if for example surgery is contemplated, because the exact location of the control for any particular function varies. The approximate area is what is known.

The cells of the brain

At the cellular level, there are two types of cells in the brain and spinal column, glial cells and neurons. The spinal column, although not considered part of the brain proper, is an extension of the brain in many ways. It is there to help transfer information back and forth between the body and the brain.

Neurons in the brain are made up of three distinct sections. At the head are the dendrites that connect to other cells. The dendrites are like tentacles that branch out from a cell body that contains one nucleus. An axon that can vary in length extends from the same cell body. There are axon terminals at the end of the axon. Axons carry nerve signals to and from the cell body.

The glial cells are very different from the neurons. They have no active part in cognition. Glia provide structure, insulation, support, and perform other functions for the neurons. Glial cells amount to about 90 percent of the cells in the brain.

Everything you have just read describes the physical components of the brain. The mind, however, is an altogether different business. As much as we tend to use the terms interchangeably, the mind and the brain are not the same thing. The brain is a tangible organ that you can touch and feel. The mind, however, is intangible, and is more of a mental construct than a physical object.

The mind uses memory and extrapolation (which can be referred to as imagination) to develop a kind of pseudo-reality inside our head. The mind uses algorithms based on occurrences in the real world and which are then extrapolated from to understand and predict future outcomes.

What we retain in our brain and the way we retain it are not exactly the way we usually think it is. All of it, including what we smell and hear, is subject to interpretation before it is stored as memory. This is true no matter how vehemently you believe that you remember things exactly the way they occurred. For instance, what we have seen with our eyes is not what we remember; rather, what we remember is an impression of what we have seen. That's how it is for most people.

The rare few who remember things exactly as they see it are described as having photographic memories. However, photographic memory can be learned and practiced. The issue isn't really about having a photographic memory, which is on one end of the spectrum, or having a processed memory, which is on the other end. The trick is to have a healthy balance of both. This doesn't mean choosing to remember some things in one way and other things in another way. Instead, it is that you remember all things in both raw or processed forms but to different degrees in two different phases of your brain.

Six hacks for the physical brain

To hack your mind, you also have to make sure that your brain is working at its best. Hacking the physical brain is fairly easy, but we rarely take the actions necessary.

If you use a little discipline to do these six things, you can supercharge the physical functioning of your brain. Do these, and you will find your brain (and mind) working better:

1. Balance your eating habits and diet.
2. Supply your brain with plenty of oxygen.
3. Drink plenty of water.
4. Sleep well.
5. Wake up before 5 a.m.
6. Get a healthy dose of sunlight every day, even in winter.

So, let's look at these more closely.

Your brain is only as good as what you eat

"You are what you eat." Everything you ingest is converted into energy, nutrients, or waste products. What is absorbed is used up or stored, and what is toxic is discarded or it accumulates. Just because something is bad for you doesn't mean all of it is excreted. Some of it remains.

You can look at it this way – if you ingested arsenic, which is highly toxic, it won't be flushed out. Instead, it is absorbed into your tissues, damaging the body at a cellular level and eventually causing death. Just because your body doesn't use something doesn't mean it is expelled from the system.

The bottom line is that everything you eat affects not only your body but also your brain. Often your brain is even more sensitive to what you ingest than the rest of your physical body.

If you eat in a healthy way, all will be well. If you eat junk, your systems deteriorate. Since this is not a book on diets, I won't go into the effects of junk food except to say that the brain deteriorates when it is fed "junk." When the physical brain deteriorates, the mind is diminished.

Most notable, however, the mind works best when it is not fueled by 100 percent glucose or glycogen. The best source of energy for the brain is a mix of ketones and glucose in a ratio between 70:30 and 80:20. Ketones are the by-product of fat metabolism. You can't take a supplement for this, but you can change the foods you eat, and how often you eat them, to trigger your body's own systems to generate ketones at moderate levels.

Ketones can replace glucose as a temporary source of fuel for the brain. Over the course of human history, we have begun consuming increasing amounts of carbohydrates which readily convert to glucose and then to fat for storage. When we give the brain a constant supply of glucose, the brain doesn't make a fuss, and just takes what it is given. It functions fairly well on glucose – but remember we aren't here to merely function, we are here to hack the mind, and to do that we should make sure that the brain is functioning at optimal levels. And the brain functions at its best when burning ketones as fuel.

If you want to learn more about ketones, Google it, or talk to someone who has adopted a ketogenic lifestyle. Otherwise, simply pay attention to how you feel when you eat carbohydrates, sugars, proteins, fats, and pay attention to how well your brain functions.

The brain needs a constant source of energy. For an organ that weighs just 2 percent of the weight of an average person (who weighs 150 pounds), it consumes more than 20 percent of the total energy the body consumes. It is the most energy-intensive organ in the body.

Also, the brain needs an energy source that is stable. In children who have poor energy profiles, experiencing repeated spikes and dips in blood sugar levels throughout the day, the brain starts to suffer, and scientists have begun to find evidence of the damage.

Researchers have found conclusive evidence that carbohydrates and high sugar diets diminish the brain's health and consequently reduce the mind's power and potential. Insulin spikes from sudden and temporary sugar highs are bad for the brain. The only way to give the brain a stable source of energy is to stop consuming carbohydrates and sugars, which are converted into glucose and glycogen, and, instead, to supply the brain with ketones which are the byproduct of metabolizing fats. Ketones are the brain's super food.

Ask any marathon runner and they will tell you that the carbohydrates they load up on are burned off less than a quarter of the way into a marathon. All the carbohydrates that are converted directly into glycogen and stored in the muscles and liver for easy access only amount to about 1,400 calories. Once that has been used up, the body's real power metabolism kicks in. All the fat that has been stored in adipose tissue all over the body begins to be metabolized. When this kicks in, runners will tell you that they feel energized, their brain gets clear, and the competitive spirit kicks in.

The brain on fat is a powerful computer. All the technology that scientists try to come up with can't even come close to what the brain can do the moment it is running in top form. The first step is to give it a stable, consistent, and powerful source of energy. When the human body eats what it naturally evolved to consume, instead of junk and processed foods, the ideal 70:30 or 80:20 ketone-to-glucose ratio is easily achieved, because of the lower amounts of glucose and carbohydrates in those foods.

If you can't follow a diet that triggers the production of ketones from fats, then, at the very least, avoid foods with a high glycemic index (GI). The glycemic index rates how quickly a food will raise the glucose level of the blood. When the blood is given a shot of glucose from eating a high GI food, insulin is released to mop it all up, causing a spike in insulin levels. Insulin is the key to moving glucose into cells where it can be converted into energy. Without insulin, glucose can't enter the cells to be converted to energy. When the body detects too much sugar in the blood, insulin is released to convert it. Two things then happen: cells take on more glucose, and insulin stops the metabolism of fat. By eating lower GI foods or foods with carbohydrates that enter the bloodstream more slowly, you can avoid that insulin spike – and avoid putting the brakes on the fat metabolism which produces those ketones that the brain functions so well on.

Get more oxygen to your brain

All of us breathe from the moment we come into this world to the moment we check out, yet nearly all of us get that simple process wrong, and pay the price for it in poor health, low energy, and less than optimal brain functioning.

Just as the brain uses 20 percent of the body's energy, the brain also uses 20 percent of the total oxygen consumed by the body. It is, by far, the largest user of oxygen among all the organs, systems, and processes of the body.

You need to ask yourself what happens when you don't get enough oxygen. The answer is that your brain gets foggy, among all the other effects that are not good for you. The typical person, especially someone who doesn't work out at least once every other day, is likely to be breathing incorrectly, resulting in insufficient oxygen intake, which means his or her brain is perpetually running on empty.

The moment you start to focus on breathing better, you will instantly see an improvement in your cognitive functioning. There are two basic ways to deliver more oxygen to the brain: breathe better, and increase circulation and absorption.

Breathe better

The first thing to do is to relearn how to breathe properly. Breathing is typically handled by the subconscious part of the brain, specifically, a part of the brain situated at the intersection of the brain and the brainstem, the medulla oblongata. This part of the brain subconsciously handles the respiration rate and even tidal breathing (breathing that occurs in a resting state).

Our body gets used to and acclimates to different conditions, even shallow breathing. The body's homeostatic mechanisms are designed to help the body acclimate to the resources available to it. If, for instance, one is placed in an oxygen-poor environment, the body would start to acclimate by shutting down various systems, and it would start to conserve resources in a way that would allow the body and brain to survive in those conditions. However, just because you can function or are surviving does not mean that you are at peak functioning.

If you are overweight, the capacity of your lungs may be restricted so that you aren't able to expand your lungs to their optimal size to take in enough oxygen to function well. Your systems will gradually begin to make do with reduced oxygen, and you acclimate to a partial hypoxic state. That reduced state includes the diminished state of your brain. If your brain is starved of oxygen, brain-related problems arise. This can present itself as foggy behavior, inaccurate analysis of issues, or even as a depressed state.

For most people, one way to gain an immediate mental edge is to start making a concerted effort to breathe better. Here are three things you can do to help yourself improve the physical act of breathing:

1. Improve your posture.

Realigning your spinal column, by sleeping on a firm surface, will help align the muscles that hold your spine in place. Then, when you are up and about, your thoracic cavity will have the optimal space available for your lungs to expand freely.

2. Reduce the size of your belly.

When your belly doesn't weigh down on your diaphragm as you sit, impinging on your diaphragm, you will improve the volume of your lung capacity.

3. Walk more.

Walking at a brisk pace deepens your breathing and strengthens your diaphragm and intercostal musculature. This allows greater breathing volume, even at rest. The increased muscle tone also allows you to deepen your breathing, increasing the volume of air that is taken in, while reducing the effort required.

The brain operates more effectively when it is receiving higher volumes of oxygen, at a more stable rate, without interruptions. However, do not force your breathing as that alters the concentration of carbon dioxide in your system and changes your oxygen intake levels.

Circulation and absorption

When we're talking about ways to improve oxygen uptake to the brain, we can't just talk about increasing the amount of oxygen we breathe in, we also need to improve the efficiency of moving that extra oxygen around the body and absorbing it into the cells where it is needed to increase cellular activity. In other words, to increase the amount of oxygen that reaches the brain, we need to improve blood circulation and the absorption of oxygen.

Circulation keeps nutrients, oxygen, and water constantly on the move so that all tissues in your body are able to get what they need to function efficiently. When one has poor circulation, oxygen doesn't get to the parts it needs to and carbon dioxide isn't removed. Waste from cellular activity remains, poisoning the surrounding tissue. Poor circulation is also a reason for the inefficient movement of particles in the blood that can eventually clog up the arteries and cause build up, eventually constricting the arteries and reducing flow of blood to the area.

In addition to circulation, the proper rate of absorption is another factor in the exchange of nutrients, oxygen, and energy in the body. Energy moves around the body in two forms, as fatty acids or glucose. Oxygen is carried by the hemoglobin in red blood cells, and nutrients are dissolved and carried in the blood.

Absorption refers to how the cells receive the energy and nutrients that have been delivered to them. Take glucose for instance. Cells do not readily absorb glucose. When the body consumes sugar, it enters the bloodstream, resulting in high levels of sugar in the blood. The sugar remains in the blood until the adrenal gland secretes insulin. That insulin attaches itself to the sugar and unlocks the cell allowing the sugar to enter. At that point, the sugar gets absorbed by the cell. Without absorption, all the food and oxygen in the world is not going to get to the cell where it is needed. That is why you need to optimize what you eat, optimize your circulation so that it all gets to where it's needed, and optimize your absorption so that once it gets there, it gets absorbed.

There are three things you can do to optimize your circulation and the absorption of the oxygen you need for peak brain functioning:

1. Drink plenty of water.
2. Increase blood volume.
3. Work out more.

1. Drink plenty of water

To keep the brain healthy and functioning at peak cognitive and mental condition, you need to keep it well hydrated. Water is essential at every step for the efficient movement and absorption of oxygen and all the other nutrients the brain relies on.

Water is the single most important component of the body, and even more so of the brain. The body is made up of 60 percent water on average, while the brain is about 73 percent water, and muscles are about 80 percent water. And that is just the water required to maintain the physical form. More water is needed to nourish, clean, lubricate, and cool the brain. All this adds up to a lot of water – both still and cycling through the body's systems. Don't think of water as something you consume to retain. Think of water as something that flows through you.

If you are drinking enough water but don't have the proper salinity levels in your system, that water is going to come right out of you without ever hydrating you at the cellular level. Without salts and electrolytes, water cannot be effectively absorbed into the cells.

The brain operates at an optimal salinity, outside of which its electrical activity diminishes drastically. Without that electrical activity there is no living brain. In fact, it is the defining quality of a living brain. A brain without electrical activity is "brain dead." It's not a stretch to say that water, salt, and electrolytes are required for a fully functioning brain and a truly "hacked" mind.

If you are concerned that you are drinking too much water, you can add hydration salts or a slice of lemon to the water you drink. That will replace electrolytes lost through perspiration or too much water intake. Mineral water is best. Avoid RO (Reverse Osmosis) water which will leech nutrients from your system and leave you worse off than before you drank it. It will also rapidly dilute the salinity across your systems.

Water is the key to optimal brain function. The healthier your brain, the more powerful your mind becomes. If you doubt the importance of water, stop drinking water for just one day and see how foggy and delirious you feel. (No, do NOT do that – I was only trying to make the point of just how critical water is to your well-being.)

Water does several things that boost the performance of your brain. Water improves cellular function and efficiency. Water acts as the "filler" in your cells to maintain their shape and keep them plumped up. It reduces the viscosity of your blood, allowing your blood to flow better. Blood plasma, which is more than half of total blood volume, is 90 percent water. Water reduces stress on the heart. If your blood is too thick, it clogs up, putting a strain on your heart, while it reduces the flow of nutrients, oxygen, and energy to everywhere, including your brain.

Water allows the efficient shuttling of toxic by-products out of the system, including out of the brain. Water also improves hepatic function. It allows the movement of toxic waste products out of the cells, tissues, and organs to the renal system. The more water you have, the more you can flush toxins out of the body, keep the brain hydrated, and keep all systems working and functioning efficiently.

2. Increase blood volume

The second thing you need to do to increase circulation and absorption of oxygen is to increase the volume of blood, specifically the volume of red blood cells. More red blood cells means a greater capacity to carry oxygen, and that increased oxygen allows for better metabolism and better brain function. The red of those blood cells is caused by haemoglobin which is an oxygen-carrying protein that contains iron.

There are a few ways to increase red blood cells in the body. A common prescription is to increase heme iron (iron from animal proteins) through dietary considerations. Iron levels can also be increased by taking supplements. Another way to increase the blood's red blood cells is to work out more.

3. Work out more

Working out more is an effective way to increase the levels of oxygen-carrying red blood cells. Physical activity that gets the heart pumping, like running or brisk walking, places a demand on the body, and to satisfy that demand, the body will adapt. One of the ways the body can adapt is to increase the production of hemoglobin to increase the blood's oxygen-carrying capacity.

Some athletes train at higher elevations where there are lower oxygen levels, so that the body is forced to adapt by increasing the production of red blood cells and dilating the capillaries and arteries. In time, those athletes adapt to the lower oxygen environment, and when they return to regular altitudes, they are able to perform better, because they can circulate more oxygen to the muscles.

But you don't need to be an athlete or climb a mountain to increase the amount of oxygen your blood can carry to your brain. The more you move physically, the more circulation you foster, so the third thing you can do to improve circulation and absorption is simply to work out more.

One way to increase something is to create the need for it. Our bodies are built to stabilize according to where we are and what we do. Athletes who train five to eight hours a day build up better muscles and better circulation to adapt to that condition of higher physical activity. That improves the circulation of oxygen- and nutrient-carrying blood, and the absorption of oxygen and nutrients, while increasing stamina, and even speeding up cognitive processes.

Sleep better

To have a fully functioning brain, you need to sleep well – and this does not necessarily mean sleeping more. In some cases, it may actually mean sleeping less. Too much sleep can cloud the brain as it reduces oxygen uptake and keeps the mind sedated for too long.

One of the most important mind hacks is the creation of an environment where your brain can form memories and extract them expeditiously. And that means sleeping well.

A lot of what we consider as having a good brain boils down to how we encode our memories. When you study something, it is of no use to you if you can't remember it or associate it with something in the past or the future. Remembering all the experiences that you go through in life is the best way to create a powerful database of knowledge, which, if encoded properly, can trigger the relevant associative memories.

When you get an idea or random memory, what is happening in the background is that one memory has been associated with another, and when you trigger one, the other is triggered as well. For people who can't control their minds that can translate into a mind in chaos.

Have you ever played the word game where your opponent says one word and you say the first thing that pops into your head? Then they say the first thing that pops into theirs, and on it goes. That is the same way your synapses fire to give you seemingly random thoughts.

Each memory is stored in a web of connections. The more connections there are to that memory, the easier it becomes to access that memory. Those connections are made while you sleep. When you make a memory while you are awake, that memory is encoded chemically by connections designed to be short-term.

To go from short-term memory to long-term memory, the chemical encoding of the memory needs to be replicated in neuronal connections. These are electro-chemical connections attached to memories that are already stored long-term in the brain. If the memory is completely new and has no relationship to what you already know, it gets harder to remember. The way we get around that is to use analogies and similes to give us a shadow of similarity which allows us to create neurons that connect to existing neurons. That's why it is always easier to understand things that are built on things we already know.

It makes sense that the more neurons there are, the better. The average brain contains a billion neurons in a lifetime. When these neurons are used, they are fortified, and more connections are made. When these neurons are not used, eventually, they are broken up and discarded. For example, if you use an access code constantly, you will remember it readily, but if you don't use it for some time, chances are that you will forget it.

The key, then, is to make as many neurons as possible, and the brain makes these neurons when we are asleep. One of the side effects of these neurons being made while we sleep is that we have dreams of randomly combined sequences. That is happening while different neurons are activated as they are being connected to the memory that is being formed.

The more neurons are connected together, the stronger the memory. And that is advanced by having more sleep. The longer you sleep, the more it promotes neurogenesis, the creation of neurons, loaded up with the memories of the day.

Sleep also helps keep the mind rested, and gives the circulation time to remove toxins that accumulate during the process of energy synthesis in the brain. Cells in the brain metabolize their own energy and this energy metabolism creates byproducts that need to be gotten rid of. Although waste products are removed gradually during the day, when you sleep, they are removed much more efficiently. That is one of the reasons you wake up "fresh" in the morning.

The quantity of time you sleep is not the only important factor in supercharging your brain and hacking your mind to do better. The time of night you sleep and the time you wake up are also important. Some of the most successful people I know have one thing in common – they all wake up before 5 a.m. or before the sun rises.

You have to find your own ideal wake up time and your ideal going to bed time. There are different guidelines that can help you figure that out. I would suggest that there are two magic numbers when it comes to sleep – four and eight. You should get either four hours of sleep or eight. I typically sleep for four hours every night between midnight and 4 a.m. When I catch the right cycle, I wake up energized and usually before the alarm goes off. Once you make it a habit, you will automatically wake up and feel energized and refreshed. Of course, the best single way to control your wake-up time is to control when you go to bed.

Get some sunshine every day

Last, but not least, expose yourself to more sunlight. We tend to underestimate the importance of sunshine in our life. Exposure to sun is responsible for supplying the body with vitamin D. Sunlight regulates the production of melatonin in the brain, which in turn regulates sleep cycles. Sunlight also causes the release of endorphins, the brain's own mood enhancing chemicals, necessary for a positive and energetic response to life. Sunlight has numerous other chemical effects on the body and brain.

The best sunlight for this is when the sun is just over the horizon, about 30 minutes after sunrise. Midday sun is fine, but it also has the highest levels of UV rays which is not good for your skin and can damage your eyes unless you are wearing eye protection. If you do go out at midday, make sure you have ample protection from harmful UV rays.

Morning sunlight, on the other hand, is something that naturally energizes and invigorates your mind. Human beings evolved to wake naturally to the bluer tones of early morning light. Many ancient traditions include morning rituals that recognize and pay tribute to the life-giving power of the earliest morning hours.

So, wake early and rise up to greet the day with a mind and brain ready to be at its best.

Afterword

The human mind is a framework based on a physical organ. It is more powerful than any contraption that the human hand can build or imagine, because the mind is the culmination of billions of minds evolving over billions of years, gradually getting better with each iteration. No CPU or computer can do better.

The reason we need to hack our mind is not that it is inadequate or faulty but because we need to find the best way to control it so it can do what it has the potential to do. That great potential is hidden under layers of distraction. From TV to constant consumerism to social media, we spend a lot of our time being persuaded to believe we are that which we are not.

Einstein, Newton, Hawking, Jobs, and countless others have had the same three-pound human brain that you and I have. Yet they made a difference only because they did the same thing you are instinctively trying to do – master the mind. "Hacking it" is really just the present era's colloquial way of expressing the same desire and intention that humankind has always had, that of bringing the mind in line with and under the direction of the *"I."*

* * *

I hope this book has brought *you* closer to *your mind*... and closer to fulfilling your dreams. Best of luck.

If you enjoyed learning how to hack your brain, I would be forever grateful if you could leave a review. Reviews are by far the best way to help authors gather valuable feedback as well as help your fellow readers find the books worth reading. Thank you so much!

www.ingramcontent.com/pod-product-compliance
Lightning Source LLC
Chambersburg PA
CBHW030057100526
44591CB00008B/188